56
Thoughts
FROM 56 HOPE ROAD

The Sayings &
Psalms of Bob Marley

56 Thoughts

FROM 56 HOPE ROAD

The Sayings &
Psalms of Bob Marley

SELECTED BY

CEDELLA MARLEY & GERALD HAUSMAN

TUFF GONG
BOOKS

Cover and text design by Ital Art
Cover photo: Dennis Morris
Text photos: Adrian Boot, Dennis Morris, Lynn Goldsmith
Lyrics: Fifty-Six Hope Road Music, Ltd./
Odnil Music, Ltd./Blue Mountain Music, Ltd.
(PRS) administered by Rykomusic, Inc. (ASCAP).

If you are unable to order this book from your
local bookseller, you may order directly from the publisher:

Tuff Gong Books
12205 Southwest 132 Court
Miami, Florida 33186, USA
tuffgongbooks@bellsouth.net

ISBN 0-9719758-0-9
10 9 8 7 6 5 4
Printed on acid-free paper in China.

LIVICATION

Let the words of our mouth
and the meditation of our hearts
be acceptable in thy sight, o FarI.

-Cedella

INTRODUCTION

Recently my children have been asking about their grandfather, and so I have written *The Boy From Nine Miles: The Early Life of Bob Marley* and now *56 Thoughts From 56 Hope Road*. This book of meditations is really like having a conversation with my dad. These are his thoughts. They are not songs – what comes out here is raw and real. And it's a personal side very few people get to see.

   Music is what it is . . . people attach themselves to it in a certain way. The spoken word is a different kind of reality. Like when he said, "Me live in the world but I'm not of the world." From that, you could say, what is going on in the world is not really for you. Because, really, you create your own world, your own safety and sanctity. And when my dad said, "I did not come to bow, I came to conquer," I think of how I am raising my own children right now. I refuse to lie. I refuse to tell my kids to believe in tooth fairies, Halloween, Columbus Day. I tell my children, Chris Columbus didn't discover Jamaica. He was the Tourist Board. So, by telling the truth about things, you are not bowing; you are conquering.

My father is such a strong presence. But we are all extensions of someone we're related to, and not related to, and that is the strong presence in us. When I do things for the benefit of my brothers and sisters, I become my father. And whether I am building an empire, physical or spiritual, I am doing it for my father. When he said, "How could you deny me my simplicity?" I think he was aware that even with all that he had accomplished, he had the right to make that statement. In truth, he didn't call himself anything. He was just who he was. Often he worked only for others. So they would have food to eat. And when he said to us, "You have no friends," what he really meant was that we had many brothers and sisters. Daddy was one man but he left an army. I think the most important thing he taught me was that nobody is beyond redemption. Nobody. He said, too, that envy is the number one killer of man. Well, my father had so much to say. Hopefully, these 56 thoughts will help you to stay upful and right.

Cedella Marley

If God didn't want me to sing,
I wouldn't have a song to sing.

Bend down low
Let me tell you
What I know.
Fisherman row,
You're going to reap
What you sow.

3

One good thing about music,
When it hits you feel no pain.

Say you just can't live
That negative way,
If you know what I mean,
Make way for that positive day.

Sun is shining
The weather is sweet.
Makes you want to move
Your dancing feet.

Hey, mister music
Sure sounds good to me.
I can't refuse it,
What to be got to be.

There's a natural mystic
Blowing through the air.
If you listen carefully now,
You will hear...
Many more will have to suffer,
Many more will have to die,
Don't ask me why.

Me don't love fighting,
But me don't love wicked either...
I guess I have a kinda war thing in me.
But is better to die fighting for freedom
Than to be a prisoner
All the days of your life.

I know I was
Born with a price on my head.

Jamaica is a place where
You build up competition in your mind.
We should all come together and
Create music and love.

How long shall
They kill our prophets
While we stand aside
And look?
Some say it's just
A part of it,
We have to fulfill the book.

And whosoever diggeth a pit
Shall fall in it.
Whosoever diggeth a pit
Shall bury in it.

13

Trodding through creation
in a irie meditation.

The road of life is rocky
And you may stumble, too.
So while you point your finger
Someone else is judging you.

Children is wonderful,
a part of my richness.

Oh let Jah love
Come shining in
Into our lives again.

The rain is falling,
And I just can't stop calling...
And I just can't tell the raindrops
From my teardrops
That's falling on my face.

Woman is to be loved
and appreciated.
Woman is an earth,
the mother of creation.
Must love woman,
but don't fall in love.
Me stand in love.
Love so much me look hungry.

I want to love you
And treat you right.
I want to love you
Every day and every night.
We'll be together with a roof
Right over our heads.
We'll share the shelter
Of my single bed.
We'll share the same room,
Jah provide the bread.

One love, one heart.
Let's get together and feel all right.
As it was in the beginning,
So it shall be in the end.

All you got to do
Is give a little,
Take a little.

Me not of the world, y'know.
Me live in the world but
I'm not of the world.

Me mustn't fight for my rights,
My rights must come to me.

I don't come to bow,
I come to conquer.

If you get up and quarrel
Every day, you're saying
Prayers to the devil, I say.

Overcome
The devils
With
A thing
Named
Love.

What we really want
Is the right to be right
And the right to be wrong.

The most intelligent people
Is the poorest people.
Yes, the thief them rich,
Pure robbers and thieves, rich!
The intelligent and innocent are poor,
Are crumbled and get brutalized. Daily.

In the beginning
Jah created everything.
He gave man dominion
Over all things.
But now it's too late,
You see, men have lost
Their faith
Eating up all the flesh
From off the earth.

Two thousand years of history
Could not be wiped away so easily.

We no know how
We and them
a-go work it out.
But someone will have to pay
For the innocent blood
That they shed
Every day
It's what the Bible say.

Destruction of the poor
Is the poverty.
Destruction of the soul
Is vanity.

33

There should be no war
between black and white!
But until white people listen to
black people with open ears,
there must be – well- suspicion.

How many rivers do we have to cross
Before we can talk to the boss?
All that we've gained we've lost.
We must've really paid the cost.

Would you let the system
Make you kill your brother man?
Would you make the system
Get on top of your head again?

36

Check out the real situation,
Nation war against nation.
Where did it all begin?
Where will it end?
Well, it seems like total destruction
Is the only solution.

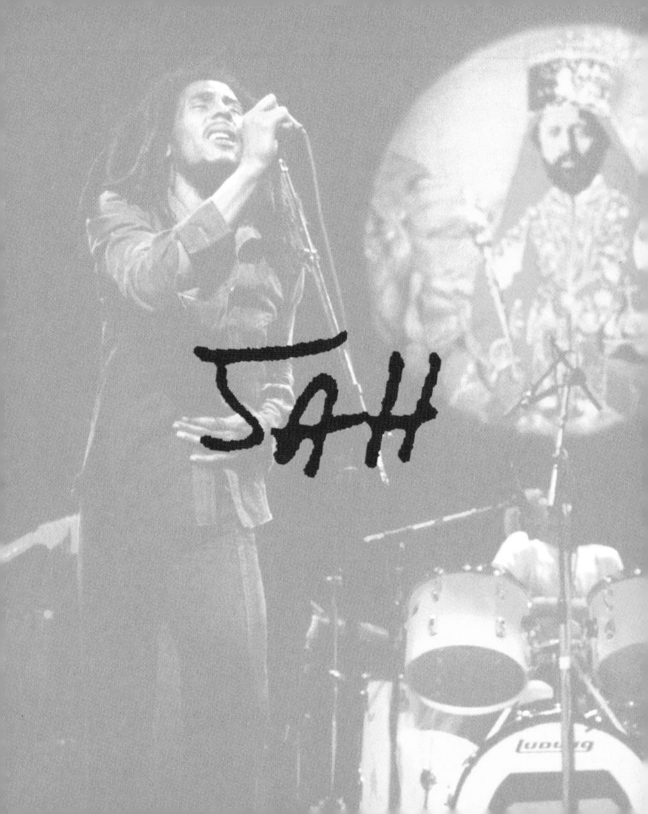
JAH

Take Jah sun
And Jah moon
And Jah rain
And Jah stars
And forever erase
Your fantasy.

Zion train is coming our way.

Every thing in life has its purpose,
Find its reason,
In every season...
We'll be forever loving Jah.

Once a man
And twice a child,
And everything
Is just for a while.

Jah appear to me in a vision
So sweet: it's me brother,
Me father, me mother, me creator,
Everything.

Selassie-I,
You can check him so.
Morning, him a baby.
Today, him a bird.
Jah live!

My music will go on forever.
Maybe it's a fool say that,
But when me know
Facts me can say facts.
My music go on forever.

What is my message?
Truth, peace and love
And music and livity.

Why do you look so sad
And forsaken?
When one door is closed
Don't you know
Another is open?

Life, it's life we deal with...
He that sees the light
And knows the light
Shall live.

One of my good friends said,
In a reggae riddim,
Don't jump in the water
if you can't swim…

There is one mystery
I just can't express.
How can you ever
Give your more
To receive your less?

Don't let them change you
Or even rearrange you.

Though my days
Are filled with sorrow,
I see there a bright tomorrow.

51

Bob Marley isn't my name,
I don't even know my name yet.

My home is in my head.

It's a foolish dog
Bark at a flying bird.
One preacher must learn
To respect the shepherd.

In high seas
Or low seas,
I'm gonna be your friend.

When the morning
Gathers the rainbow
Want you to know
I'm a rainbow, too.

I've been here before
And will come again.